Original title:
Where the Walls Speak

Copyright © 2025 Creative Arts Management OÜ
All rights reserved.

Author: Julian Prescott
ISBN HARDBACK: 978-1-80587-121-7
ISBN PAPERBACK: 978-1-80587-591-8

Shadows of Forgotten Lives

In corners, whispers giggle light,
Where shadows dance in the moon's bright.
They tell tales of socks lost in the fray,
And the cats plotting mischief to play.

Old fixtures chuckle, barely awake,
Recalling the pranks that caused quite a shake.
A knock on the door? It's just the wind!
With a creaky laugh, let the fun begin!

Echoing Footsteps of Yesteryear

Footsteps tap-dance on creaky floors,
Mimicking the clatter of opening doors.
Echoes of laughter bounce off the wall,
Inviting old secrets to have a ball.

A cat runs past, tail high, so proud,
Chasing a ghost that giggles aloud.
They reminisce about spilled drinks and fun,
And awkward dance moves, all one by one.

The Lament of Painted Walls

The walls wear colors, chipped and bright,
Their stories hang on, an amusing sight.
They sigh of the times paint was splattered,
Over a cake-baking fail, oh how it mattered!

With a pitter-patter, the rain begins,
Tickling the roof, sparking giggles and grins.
As colors blend, what a charming war,
Of drips and dribbles that call for encore!

Secrets Shared by the Ceiling

Up high, the ceiling shares its lore,
Of late-night snacks and blocks of four.
Heat from the lamp casts shadows sly,
As it has witnessed each pie in the sky.

Cobwebbed corners hold things untold,
Of daring adventures, both silly and bold.
As time drips down through cracks and seams,
It spins yarns of laughter and wild dreams.

Resonance of the Facade

A statue winked when no one looked,
His secrets buried, mildly cooked.
The paint peels off, it's quite a sight,
And whispers giggle deep in the night.

The cobblestones, they dance around,
In slushy boots, we all fall down.
The walls chuckle, knowing our plight,
As we trip on bricks in pure delight.

Monuments of Memory

Old pictures hang with crooked grins,
While silly tales drum up like violins.
A vase of flowers sneezes in flair,
As dust bunnies burst from their lair.

Ghosts of laughter roam through the halls,
Throwing parties that nobody calls.
With poltergeist pranks, they take a chance,
Adding jiggles to every dance.

The Breath of the Room

Socks tumble freely in a wild spree,
While coats play hide-and-seek with glee.
The air is thick with ticklish dust,
As curious spiders weave their must.

Chairs are gossiping about the cat,
Who snagged a snack and wore it flat.
With every creak, the jokes unfold,
In corners where mysteries are told.

Echoing Dreams of the Past

A clock strikes twelve, but it's quite wrong,
Singing soft tunes as we hum along.
The old piano laughs in its keys,
As memories dance on the whispering breeze.

In the attic, a trunk full of hats,
Plans for parties with invisible cats.
Each item perched on history's lap,
Has stories to share in a playful clap.

Fables in the Framework

In the corner a mouse tried to dance,
He stepped on a cat, didn't stand a chance.
The cat just sighed, rolled over to snooze,
And the mouse laughed hard, in a playful ruse.

A nail poked its head out, quite keen to jest,
It told a tall tale of a drawing contest.
The hammer was blushing, it couldn't compete,
With a nail art disaster no one could beat!

Lyrical Landscapes of the Everyday

The fridge hums a tune, a curious song,
It's debating with butter, who's right or wrong.
Celery pipes in, all crunchy and proud,
Till the pickles chime in, all sour and loud.

On the table a spoon had a dramatic flair,
It dreamed of being fancy, but just held the chair.
A fork rolled its eyes, with a life on the run,
Together they laughed, oh what silly fun!

The Chronicles of Companionship

Two chairs in the sun, they gossip and sway,
One's got a crack that just won't go away.
The other laughs hard, saying it's just a scar,
And shows off its fabric, all ripped by the bar.

A dog wanders close, with a sniff and a bark,
Asking why they're so funny, perched there in the park.
The chairs just chuckle, old friends in a spin,
"Life's a wild ride, come join in the din!"

Regrets Etched in Mortar

A timeworn brick sighed, with stories to share,
Of builders who laughed, but forgot how to care.
They dropped their own tools, and that made a mess,
Now the wall's got a crack, oops, what a stress!

In shadows they linger, the echoes of yore,
Married to laughter, and maybe a sore.
A plaster pitied the bricks in their plight,
"Just remember," it chuckled, "your humor's still bright!"

Unheard Tales of the Hearth

In the corner, a kettle whistled loud,
Secret gossip from a steaming crowd.
The cat rolled its eyes at the empty chair,
Claiming it's home, with a sassy flair.

The toaster chimed in, cracking a joke,
About the bread, it desperately stroked.
Each crumb tells a tale, a comical quest,
In this lively home, they never rest.

Legends of the Forgotten

In dusty corners, the legends crawl,
A sock puppet queen holds court, enthralled.
She fights with a spoon, a showdown bright,
As imaginary knights join in the fight.

Old shoes laugh, as they recount their trips,
A journey that ended with numerous slips.
Each tale is a giggle, a memory dear,
Echoing softly, 'Oh, bring us a beer!'

The Heartbeat of Old Beams

The beams in the ceiling creak and moan,
As if they recall the laughter they've sown.
A dance party for dust, they twirl in delight,
While the moths are the guests inflating the night.

Charming whispers float from the hearth, so warm,
Reminding the spoons to avoid the barnstorm.
Against the old wood, a new joke is framed,
In a world where no wood ever feels shamed.

Chronicles of the Dust

A dusty old tome lies quietly still,
Filled with stories that give quite a thrill.
It chuckles at spiders that spin webs on the shelf,
'You're collecting my history, but take it yourself!'

A tumbleweed scoffs, with bravado profound,
'I'm the king of the hallway, just look at me bound!'
Each pile holds a secret, a story unspun,
As they revel in nonsense, oh what fun has begun!

Canvases of Christian Homes

In kitchens bright with apple pie,
Some secrets bubble, oh my, oh my!
A cat on the counter, a dog on the floor,
Heard laughter echo, but oh, what a roar!

Grandma's china, a stories' delight,
Meant for the table, not for a fight!
A spoon goes flying, a pie takes a dive,
Just another tale, where all families thrive!

Whispers of Wisdom in Weathered Wood

In the creaky floorboards, the past has a say,
As Grandpa's old chair tries to sneak away.
The wooden beams chuckle at ghosts from the past,
Scripted with laughter, they'll forever last.

Nails and knots hold stories of cheer,
Like a squirrel on a mission, it's quite sincere!
They gossip in whispers, while dust bunnies twirl,
Navigating life like a child with a pearl.

Resonating Rhythms of Residence

In a hall where the clock tick-tocks with glee,
Time dances funny, like a bumblebee.
The echoes of footsteps, a marathon, indeed,
Who's racing for snacks? It's a wild stampede!

Echoing laughter, the walls cannot lie,
The distance between them and a pie in the sky!
Swinging laughs bounce in a color parade,
As socks find their matches, but they seem afraid.

Tones of Tapestries Left Untold

Tapestries woven with colors so bright,
Spin tall tales of a cat's daring flight.
The dog on the couch makes a pirate's decree,
As birds sing a tune of sweet jubilee.

Each angle a canvas of long-lost fun,
With whimsical patterns that never are done.
The tangled yarn whispers of good times ahead,
While knitting a story that never gets thread.

Reflections in the Grime

In corners lurk some old dust mites,
They gossip about our late night bites.
A cluttered shelf, a hidden tale,
Of mismatched socks that start to pale.

The fridge hums loud, a grumpy tune,
It remembers pasta left too soon.
Each bite of cake, there's laughter spread,
From crumbs that dance where we once tread.

The Ghosts of Living Spaces

A chair that squeaks, it cracks a joke,
'The cat can't sit; she'd rather poke!'
The lamp flickers, winks at the wall,
'In this house, I'm standing tall!'

The table relays tales of clumsiness,
From spilled drinks to friends in messiness.
Old coats hang, they share their dreams,
Of wild nights out and ice cream themes.

Beneath the Surface

Underneath the floorboards creak,
Rats hold court and start to speak.
They riff on cheese and scary sights,
And keep track of our late-night bites.

The rug whispers secrets from the past,
Of big family dinners, fun to last.
It laughs at us when we trip and fall,
'Just join the dance, it's a ball after all!'

They Speak

The pipes gurgle with a sassy flair,
'Tell me again, why's there hair everywhere?'
The toilet hums a soft refrain,
Of plopping down with a dubious gain.

Windows giggle, catching the sun,
'Watching you fumble is quite the fun!'
The walls hear all with patient grace,
They know every joke, every face.

Letters Written in Brick

Brick by brick, stories unfold,
Of pizza nights and friends so bold.
They form a wall, but also a friend,
With each scratch, a laugh to lend.

Each crack a line of silly prose,
Echoes of lives and funny woes.
In every crevice, a jest is tucked,
'Naps are vital,' the couch just plucked.

Heartstrings of the Hearth

In the corner, a chair with a frown,
Leaves crumbs of laughter spread all around.
Touts tales of the socks that once played,
In a dance of the mischievous parade.

The pot on the stove begins to hum,
Singing secrets of sauce and plum.
Cookies whisper, 'We're almost done!'
They don't care who's lost, or who's won.

Unveiling the Hidden Inhabitants

Beneath the floor, the dust bunnies prance,
Throwing a party, inviting the ants.
They gossip and giggle, oh what a sight!
Planning a feast under the moonlight.

The ceiling creaks with a chuckle and sigh,
As shadows debate who's the funniest guy.
A ghost pulls a prank, oh, what a tease,
'Boo!' he shouts, 'Did I scare you, please?'

Soliloquies of the Settled

Chairs converse over old, wrinkled news,
While lamps share their glow, in colorful hues.
The cat rolls his eyes at their chatter and tales,
While plotting his course for the windowsills' pales.

The coffee pot chimes in with a gurgle so keen,
'I'm brewing up laughter, you know what I mean?'
And curtains wave softly, with giggles in drift,
In this cozy dwelling, they're the jokesters adrift.

Echoes in the Empty Hall

The hallway chuckles with every tread,
As shoes slip and slide, making merry instead.
Echoes of laughter dance on the breeze,
Hiding their glee behind squeaky keys.

A ghost in a sheet plays tag with the dust,
Chasing light beams, in a game of trust.
Back and forth, they flip and flop,
Whoever gets caught must take a stop!

The Language of Shadows

In the corner, shadows dance,
They tell jokes, and take a chance.
A ghostly wink, a playful jest,
They're the life of the unseen fest.

Oh, a wall exclaimed, "Check my new hue!"
"It's a shade I borrowed, just for you!"
Laughter echoes, through the old hall,
Even bricks have fun, after all!

A cheeky crack shared a pun,
"I'm breaking up, just for fun!"
The plaster giggled, "Don't be shy,
Let's have a laugh before we dry!"

The ceiling chuckled with a squeak,
"Who knew walls could be such freaks?"
In the realm of paint and debris,
A fiesta of whispers was all you could see.

Conversations of the Void

In a quiet nook, the void does chat,
"Did you hear that?" said a lazy rat.
"The walls have tales of odd names,
Like Morty the Moth and Priscilla the Flames!"

A corner replied, with a dramatic flair,
"I once saw a sock, without a pair!"
Echoes burst forth, with giggles galore,
Of missing things and what's in store.

A lightbulb flickered, straining to see,
"I need a break; this gossip's not free!"
But the void insisted, in a charming way,
"Stay for the punchline, it's really okay!"

From the depths of silence, laughter arose,
As shadows entangled in happy prose.
In a world where giggles never fade,
Even the empty finds their trade.

Secrets in the Cracks

There's a crack in the wall, with stories to spill,
"Come closer," it whispers, with a chuckle and thrill.
"Did you hear about Timmy, the crafty old rat?
He stole all the snacks and danced like a brat!"

The floorboards creaked, in a fit of delight,
"Was that Timmy I saw, sneaking at night?"
Paint peeled back, with a knowing grin,
"Every good tale must begin with a sin!"

A chip laughed, "I was here long before,
When paint was fresh, and no one kept score.
Let's share our secrets, let's have our say,
The silliness here, it will never decay!"

The room embraced its charming quirks,
With secrets caught in its sneaky perks.
In every crevice, joy did unite,
As the walls held court, on that merry night.

Murmurs of the Abandoned

In an old house where laughter's a ghost,
The beams tell tales, that we love the most.
"Remember the kitten?" a window chimed,
"It knocked over flowers, how we all laughed and primed!"

A door creaked softly, sharing a grin,
"Tales of a slumber party, where no one could win!
With pillows as weapons, and snacks on the run,
We fought for the title of 'Best Pudding Fun!'"

The attic mumbled, dust dancing in flight,
"Hey, let's reminisce, over cookies tonight!
With cobwebs and clatter, we'll throw a bash,
To celebrate memories in a wondrous flash!"

In corners untouched, the laughter held strong,
For even in silence, there's always a song.
Abandoned, yet busy, they cast their own spell,
In the echo of fun, where the whispers dwell.

Chronicles in the Corners

In the corner, a sock appears,
A tale of laundry, laughs, and cheers.
Dust bunnies gossip, what a sight,
Chasing each other in the moonlight.

Old chairs creak and share their woes,
Voices from times that nobody knows.
They spread their rumors, oh what fun,
Like a sitcom, they're never done.

A picture frame winks with glee,
Telling stories of you and me.
With every creak, a punchline lands,
Life's a joke; it's all unplanned.

So if you hear them laugh at night,
Join the chorus; it's pure delight.
The corners hold secrets, laughter spins,
In this circus, everyone wins.

Echoes of Forgotten Dreams

In the attic, shadows sway,
Old dreams dance in a funny way.
A teddy bear with a giddy grin,
Tries to remember where it's been.

A stack of boxes, memories piled,
Each one filled with antics, wild.
The echoes giggle, a light surprise,
Whispers of joys that never die.

Old records play a silly tune,
While dust motes twirl like a cartoon.
Forgotten wishes bob and weave,
In this place, it's hard to grieve.

So come and listen, take a peek,
In every corner, laughter speaks.
The hidden joys, they gently beam,
In a world stitched from a dream.

The Soul of the Shelter

Beneath the roof, a playful breeze,
The walls chuckle with the trees.
Each room holds a riddle wide,
A ticklish nook where joys collide.

The cupboard creaks, a jar falls down,
And spills the marbles, oh what a clown!
In every whimper, a giggle grows,
The spirit of shelter, it overflows.

A pop-tart cat stares down the hall,
With sass and snickers, he has it all.
Chasing shadows, he prances about,
Life's a joke, without a doubt.

So gather 'round, your troubles shed,
The walls embrace, just like a bed.
In this haven, joy's the rule,
Where laughter reigns, we're always cool.

Breaths of the Abiding Walls

The walls whisper secrets, giggles snort,
Every crack holds a funny sort.
A tickle here, a poke there too,
Oh, what nonsense they'll share with you!

In every sound, a punchline hides,
Radiating joy from all sides.
The wallpaper winks, what a sly tease,
While the light flickers with comic ease.

In the hallway, echoes chase the cat,
With every leap, a laugh comes flat.
A lightbulb flickers, a quick little joke,
And the entire room bursts into smoke!

So let's embrace the humor within,
The walls remember every whim.
Together we thrive, life's comic ball,
Join the laughter in the rise and fall.

The Song of Silent Spaces

In the corner a chair, a cat, and a bear,
Sipping on tea with an invisible flair.
They gossip and giggle, oh what a pair,
While the dust bunnies dance without any care.

A mouse in a bow tie conducts with great glee,
As the spoons and the forks join in harmony.
They toot and they twang, a delightful decree,
Even the light bulb hums a sweet symphony.

The walls arch their backs to lean in and hear,
Every chuckle and snicker, a whimsical cheer.
With secrets they cherish, they play it all clear,
In their quirky domain, laughter is near.

So come take a peek, and don't make a sound,
Listen closely, for joy does abound.
In these silent realms where the fun can be found,
The spirit of humor forever is crowned.

Echos of the Ether

In an attic so dusty, with whispers so bold,
Rats in pajamas spin stories retold.
They glide on the beams, they dance and unfold,
Painting pictures of laughter with nothing but mold.

A ceiling fan squeaks, laughing along,
Strumming tunes from the past, a curious song.
With socks on the ceiling, what could go wrong?
Join the party of echoes where humor is strong.

The windows, they chime in with pitter-pat jokes,
As squirrels in top hats entertain with their hoaxes.
The only real rule is: keep laughing, folks!
For the fun is eternal, and joy never chokes.

So listen, you might find a playful refrain,
In the corners of the air, through the sunlight and rain.
Where echoes collide, it's simply insane,
A whimsical haven where laughter's not plain.

Echoes in the Silence

A cactus named Spike played tag with the air,
He teased with a poke, but it didn't seem fair.
The shadows just chuckled, a smirk they would wear,
For in the dusk quiet, hilarity's flare.

The whispers of curtains all flapped in delight,
As a curtain rod danced on a glorious night.
Candles watched closely, their flames shining bright,
They'd never guess walls can giggle with might.

A mouse with a top hat held court and proclaimed,
That silence, my friends, has often been blamed.
For humor and giggles are easily tamed,
When the walls start to chat, and jokes are unframed.

So tiptoe through echoes where laughter holds reign,
Dive into riddle, enjoy every strain.
For in these odd moments, where fun's not a bane,
Lives a kingdom of jest, spiraling insane.

Whispers of the Stone

In a garden of pebbles, a stone throws a fit,
He claims he's a diamond, never to split.
Though rough around edges, he won't ever quit,
With wit that astounds, he doesn't need grit.

Amidst all the flowers, a rock will recite,
Old tales of the dirt, with smiles pure and bright.
The worms all nod softly, they're charmed by the sight,
As the petals lean in, it's a giggle-filled night.

The bricks on the path join with laughter and cheer,
As they shimmy and sway, they've nothing to fear.
In the rhythm of nature, the humor is clear,
These whispers of stone sing what hearts long to hear.

So stroll through this garden, let joy be your guide,
For cracks in the sidewalk might let laughter slide.
With whispers exploding, no reason to hide,
In a world filled with chuckles, let happiness ride.

Stories Etched in Time

In the corners, laughter hides,
With tales of socks and garden slides.
A dance with dust, a twirl with care,
As echoes of giggles float in the air.

Old frames wiggle, pictures sway,
While a cat sneaks by, in her ballet.
The wallpaper peels with a knowing grin,
As memories jump on the record spin.

A fridge hums tales of leftovers bold,
Whispers of parties, secrets untold.
The chair creaks in a rhythm bright,
Holding stories of every late night.

About that time things went a-miss,
She danced on a table and stole a kiss.
The walls remember, they chuckle too,
At the antics we thought no one knew.

The Hushed Testimony

Behind the paint, a chorus sings,
Of teddies, toys, and slippery swings.
Muffled giggles that rise and fall,
While daydreams tumble and hide in the hall.

The ceiling fans spin yarns so tall,
About penguins playing billiards in the hall.
Above the mantle, a sly grin waits,
As the clock winks at our messy fates.

A cactus nods, its needles slack,
Swaying to stories of the great snack attack.
The lamp flickers tales of silly feats,
As the carpet plots a dance with my feet.

Nothing's quiet when the night creeps in,
As tales flip pages on a whim.
In the hush, we find our spree,
In whispers of all that used to be.

Voices Beneath the Plaster

The walls hum with a giddy cheer,
Of paintball fights and strong-rooted fear.
A smudge of ketchup, a splatter of cake,
Dining room memories that make us awake.

Bass thuds softly from yonder room,
As curtains sway to a humorous tune.
Each chip in the plaster tells a tale,
Of two left feet and dramatic fails.

Chairs bicker about who sat where,
While the floorboards squeak with a wink and a stare.
A mouse in the cupboard steals crumbs with glee,
And giggles join in, as wild as can be.

Each shadow a player in this merry game,
A race around corners, no one's the same.
Lost in the laughter, amid the jest,
This is home, we're truly blessed.

Silence Within the Structure

In corners, you'd catch a sly snicker,
From a shy spectator, the wooden sticker.
The light bulb's flicker, it knows what's up,
As rogue socks dance in a jumbled cup.

Columns that echo with whispers of cheer,
About that one time we danced on a deer.
Brushes of laughter paint stories anew,
While chandeliers swing with a comedic view.

The door creaks gossip that stirs the night,
Between sips of tea, oh what a sight!
Silly arguments that come and go,
Each round a jest, a friendly show.

Though silence rests, it's far from bland,
Each crack and crease gives a helping hand.
In this playful haven, we laugh and mend,
The walls support, they even lend.

Dreams Entombed in Timber

In a house that sways and creaks,
Wooden beams reveal their secrets.
The ghosts of dreams long past still laugh,
While the mice throw their own little party.

A squirrel snickers from the eaves,
As memories dance on old wood floors.
Whispers echo like fading chimes,
Tickling ears and causing snorts.

Picture frames wiggle with delight,
As the wind plays jester with curtains.
The shampoo bottles on the shelf smile,
Laughing at combs who've lost their way.

A door creaks open, just for fun,
A playful breeze chats with the rafters.
Timber keeps its stiff upper lip,
While the house hosts a soirée of chatter.

Harmony of History and Habitat

Walls hold tales, a raucous crew,
Where blueprints battle old flues.
An attic's yarn spun from the past,
Tickles the floor in a wiggle blast.

Each brick hums with memories clear,
Of disco balls and squeaky cheers.
Nooks burst with laughter and light,
As shadows sneak in for the night.

Curtains flap like they're in on a joke,
While the fridge hums a tuneful poke.
Pictures whisper sweet little lies,
As the clock rolls its eyes and sighs.

A rug responds with a little dance,
To the rhythm of happy circumstance.
In this space where echos merge,
History waltzes while ruins surge.

Dialogues of the Dwellings

The walls chat over morning tea,
Cracking jokes, oh, how they agree!
A chair shimmies with playful glee,
While the lamp rolls its eyes like a flea.

Windows wink, catching sunshine bright,
They gossip with curtains, oh what a sight!
A clock ticks along with cheeky flair,
Setting the mood for a laugh affair.

On the shelf, dusty relics cheer,
Outdated stories they hold dear.
Candles flicker as if to say,
"Join the fun, come out and play!"

A cupboard joins in with a thud,
An unexpected voice in the flood.
Together they weave a tapestry,
Of silliness and pure jubilee.

The Resonance of Relics

In corners, echoes crackle and pop,
A relics' meeting, they'll never stop.
From spoons to bowls, stories collide,
In this chamber where laughter won't hide.

A vase giggles, tipping with charm,
While the bookends talk about farm.
A statue grins in well-dressed flair,
As walls lean in to catch the air.

Old toys chatter of yesteryears,
Tickling dust that somehow still cheers.
An exasperated broom grumbles and sweeps,
While history lingers and softly peeps.

Chairs rattle with pleasantries sweet,
As the floor becomes a musical beat.
Relics unite for the ultimate fare,
In a living room full of laughter and care.

Stories Concealed in the Plaster

Once upon a time, a nail did confide,
In the laughter of walls where secrets reside.
With whispers from paint, they giggled out loud,
Sharing tales of dust and a long-absent crowd.

There's a story of mice and their late-night feast,
Who danced on the beams like a wild little beast.
The coffee stain's gossip, oh what a delight,
Revealing the chaos from parties at night.

A crack in the corner held treasures untold,
A sock and an old toy, both dusty and bold.
With the scent of old echoes, they chuckled in glee,
What a riot it is to hear walls talk, you see!

So next time you're near a drab, silent hall,
Just listen a bit, they might entertain all.
For laughter's the glue, it'll make time a breeze,
The stories they hold can bring anyone to knees!

The Symphony of Structure

There once was a house with a quirk in its frame,
Its beams hummed a tune, never quite the same.
Each creak told a story, a melodic twist,
Where woodwinds of laughter would often persist.

The floorboards would tap dance, delightful and spry,
As chandeliers swayed in a whimsical sigh.
Oh, the windows would wink while they gleamed in the sun,
In an orchestra grand, every detail had fun!

The chimney would puff in a rhythm that swayed,
Chasing off smoke while it expertly played.
The roof might just sigh with a gentle refrain,
As showering raindrops brought music like rain.

So listen closely, don't let the quiet fool,
For the home is a stage with its own playful rule.
A symphony wild, where laughter takes flight,
In the harmony of a house, joy ignites.

Resonance of Resilient Edges

In the corners so sharp, the bricks often sang,
Of barbecues burned and the laughter that rang.
The paint would rejoice with a tickle and tease,
Making memories dance on a breath of warm breeze.

Oh, the sassy old tile would flirt with the floor,
While dust bunnies twirled, craving just a bit more.
Walls draped in echoes, infectious, amiable,
Crafting moments of mirth, just a tad whimsical.

Meanwhile, the roof with a sly little grin,
Hoped raindrops would laugh as they danced on its skin.
Each shingle was grateful for summers so light,
Together they'd sing in the soft, silvery night.

So heed the structure, it's built with a flair,
It holds all the giggles, the sighs in the air.
In resilient shadows, the joy it won't cage,
Just listen and revel in each funny page!

Dialogues of Dusty Cornerstones

Gather 'round, dear friends, let the stories unfold,
In the corners of homes where the brave tales are told.
The stones have opinions, they've seen quite the show,
Debating old secrets with a smirk, don't you know?

"Hey, did you see that?" the left stone would say,
"Last winter's snowfall, what a splendid display!"
The right stone would chuckle, "Oh, I'd never forget,
The time that old cat left us all in a fret!"

A chat in the twilight, the mosquitoes all buzz,
They chuckle at memories, just because, just because!
Each pebble is hearty, no dullness allowed,
As laughter drips down from the clouds overhead.

So lend them your ear, these wise stones of the place,
Experience the joy in their rough, textured grace.
With humor and heart, and a wink of the eye,
In dusty dialogues, life's treasures go by!

Reflections on Rough Surfaces

In the cracks, a peek of a mouse,
Sneaky in his tiny house.
The plaster sighs in tales, no doubt,
Of awkward moments, all about.

A scuff reveals a secret dance,
Of feet that tripped, with no romance.
Chipped paint whispers of wild nights,
With laughter echoing in bites.

Walls blush when secrets they keep,
Underneath, they giggle and peep.
Echos of the past tickle the air,
As dust bunnies gossip with flair.

Each mark a story, each smudge a laugh,
A comedic script in a drafty path.
Rough surfaces, a canvas divine,
Full of quirks, and oh, how they shine!

The Palette of Painted Voices

Colors clash like zany sports,
Each hue plays host to funny reports.
The green says, 'I'm not just for grass!',
While purple brags, 'I'm never last!'

Red giggles with a sassy tint,
Claiming it's the world's favorite hint.
Yellow beams like a sunny smile,
While blue reminds it's the calmest style.

Brushes dip in laughter's stew,
Painting chatter in every hue.
A canvas bright with tales untold,
As vibrant whispers begin to unfold.

The palette hums a merry tune,
Under the watch of a playful moon.
Voices of colors, bold and free,
Creating a joke in harmony!

Fables of Foundation and Frame

The floor creaks out a funny joke,
About a cat who tried to croak.
The beams above quip with a grin,
'That's not how you get a win!'

The foundation laughs with a rumble,
At all the kids who love to tumble.
While windows wink, conspirators wise,
Hiding secrets with playful sighs.

Every corner holds a giggle,
In the frame, an amusing wiggle.
A tale told in the blink of a door,
Of past lives that are never a bore.

As stories rise up like craft in the air,
Foundations hold truths with flair.
In this home where laughter remains,
Walls tell tales through goofy refrains!

Riddles of the Roof

The shingles chatter in the breeze,
Sharing riddles with the trees.
'What's heavy but can't be seen?'
'The weight of a bad pun, keen and mean.'

Overhead, clouds chuckle and roll,
As raindrops drop in a comic shoal.
While twinkling stars play hide and seek,
Whisper jokes to the moon and peek.

Each ridge a tale, each slope a song,
For critters that dart all day long.
The echoing laughter from up high,
Makes even the sky laugh and sigh.

Under this roof of whimsical dreams,
Reality is stitched with funny seams.
So let every riddle make you grin,
In this world where giggles begin!

Fables of the Fading Light

In the corner a shadow does dance,
Telling tales of socks lost by chance.
With giggles and whispers, it takes a stand,
As the curtains sway, it waves its hand.

The chandelier chuckles, its crystals all twinkled,
A squeaky old floorboard just slightly crinkled.
Lively discussions with dust bunnies roam,
While the clock ticks softly, they call it home.

A painting winks, its colors all bright,
As the cat spins webs in the glow of night.
A mouse in a hat starts to waltz with pride,
While brewing up stories the bugs can't abide.

At dusk, all the corners come out to play,
With secrets and laughter, they brighten the way.
A tapestry hums of adventures untold,
In this fun little realm, with each fold unfolds.

The Hidden Chronicles of Corners

Behind every nook, a story must wait,
With gnomes and their hats forming quite the fate.
A tablecloth grumbles of spills it has seen,
While the broom in the corner just sweeps in between.

The candles giggle in flickering light,
As the wallpaper whispers, "I've seen quite the sight!"
There's a friendly old mirror who tries to reflect,
On the antics of laughter, and all they neglect.

A welcome mat murmurs of shoes that don't match,
While the doorknob chuckles, a twist is his catch.
"Oh, the shenanigans that unfold every day,
In this room of odd tales where sunlight holds sway!"

With echoes of laughter stuck up on the shelf,
Each corner a character, all full of itself.
Forming a cast of the quirkiest kin,
In a stage made of shadows, where smiles always win.

Timeless Whispers of Clay

The potter's wheel spins with giggles and glee,
As the clay dreams of shapes it hopes to be.
A vase rolls its eyes, feeling quite round,
While the bowls crack up with a comical sound.

The kiln softly murmurs, "Please do not shout,"
As a mug makes a plea, "I am not a clout!"
With each swirl and twist, a vessel is born,
Tales of the pinch pots and mishaps are worn.

As the plates stack high, they throw quite a fit,
Saying, "We're not just plates, we're the life of the skit!"
With spoons in a swirl and forks in a dance,
Each piece shares a chuckle, a whimsical chance.

In this land made of clay, where laughter is spun,
With smiles in the glaze, every piece is a pun.
A cup raises its handle for all to toast,
To the timeless old whispers that laughter loves most.

The Unseen Chronicles

In the attic, a trunk laughs with mystery's air,
With old clothes rejoicing, they show off their flair.
A skirt sways in rhythm, a dress takes a twirl,
As the hats trade old stories in a floppy swirl.

Beneath the old stairs, the dust motes engage,
In soft, gentle discussions like winds on a page.
While the paintings above peek with curious eyes,
And the curtains get frisky with playful sighs.

The old radio hums of tunes from the past,
As the records spin tales that are meant to last.
A clock chimes in laughter—"Time's just a game!"
And the memories dance, though they're never the same.

In this whimsical place where secrets do bloom,
Each crevice and corner brings joy to the room.
With unseen chronicles that bring laughter's embrace,
All the stories collide, a comical space.

The Anatomy of a Residence

In the corner, a couch sighs,
Once proud, now home to lost fries.
A lamp flickers, playing hide and seek,
While shadows dance, the floors creak.

The fridge hums a tune so sweet,
Stocked with leftovers, a feast for the fleet.
Plates whisper tales of past dinner fights,
As forks and spoons share midnight bites.

Upstairs, the cat makes a grand debut,
Leaping from shelves like it always knew.
The walls giggle at secrets long stored,
While dust bunnies plot their next hoard.

A clock ticks away, a metronome's prank,
Time's a joker, painting walls blank.
In this house of laughter and strange decor,
Every corner grins, begging for more.

Silhouettes of Sorrow

In the hallway, a shadow vanishes,
Was it a ghost or just palishes?
A mirror reflects a dance of the sad,
But the goldfish thinks it's just a fad.

Chairs sit idle, nibbling on dust,
Comfy and plush, but not always just.
They whisper softly of tales once grand,
Of parties missed and the few that planned.

A clock bears witness to time's funny taunt,
It chimes for laughs, but knows what will haunt.
Potted plants eavesdrop on every sigh,
Sipping on sunlight, wondering why.

But laughter bubbles under tension thick,
As the walls groan from every trick.
A tickle of joy hides in the grey,
As echoes of sadness skip away.

Paths of Presence and Absence

In the kitchen, a ghost seems to bake,
Cookies of silence, for goodness' sake!
The oven's preheated, but who will taste?
Maybe the cat, with impeccable haste.

A hallway stretches, a limbo of sorts,
With shoes misplaced, like autumn sports.
They trip on shadows, these sneaky little things,
And tumble through laughter that the silence brings.

The closet, a circus of coats on parade,
Whispers of winter, a woolly charade.
When breezes sneak in, they ruffle the seams,
Shaking off memories and lingering dreams.

But here in the gaps, joy plays peek-a-boo,
Hallways and nooks sip on moments so new.
A playful reminder that all can switch lanes,
In paths where absence and presence reigns.

The Essence of Abiding

In the living room, the TV sighs,
Next to potted plants with watching eyes.
The remote control, a distant crown,
Hopes for laughter whenever it's found.

Windows open wide to catch the breeze,
Negotiating peace with rustling trees.
Yet, papers flutter, gossiping away,
About the mischief they saw in the fray.

Light bulbs wink like they know the score,
While sofas pillow "What's life for?"
Each creak in the floor, a subtle jest,
In this kingdom of comfort, it's all a fest.

Though time may age the tales that we weave,
In laughter and joy, we continue to believe.
The essence of our days finds a place to abide,
And within these walls, our joy does not hide.

The Legacy of Walls Unseen

Brick and mortar, they keep it all,
Laughing echoes in every hall.
Hushed whispers from the paint so bright,
Tales of mishaps, both day and night.

Chasing shadows, a game of hide,
While creaky floorboards take a ride.
Imaginary friends from days of yore,
Share old secrets and ask for more.

Nail holes laughing, quite the crowd,
Cheering memories, so proud and loud.
They witness joy, they witness strife,
In quiet corners, they breathe our life.

From sticky fingers to cake in the air,
These walls chuckle at our silly flair.
With every stumble, every tear,
They'll guard our mischief, year after year.

Memories Carved in Time

Dusty shelves hold stories galore,
Spilled secrets, a floor that swore.
Crammed with mischief, mismatched shoes,
In every crack, there's laughter to lose.

Paint peels like a faded grin,
Ticklish moments, where do I begin?
Scribbles on the walls, our little names,
Reminding us of childhood games.

Peepholes to adventures gone past,
A treasure trove of giggles that last.
Echoes of laughter in every nook,
Retracing steps in this quirky book.

Tales of the cat that danced in the night,
Or the best hide-and-seek that felt just right.
Memories wax and wane like the sun,
Captured forever, oh what fun!

Gossamer Threads of Unspoken Words

Whispers in corners, just out of sight,
Giggling secrets that take flight.
Spider webs spin tales in the gloom,
As shadows sway, they dance in the room.

Tick-tock of laughter on a wall's thin skin,
Walls hold the punchlines, we just grin.
Hiccups and slip-ups, the fumbles we made,
They weave our stories, delicately laid.

Echoes of fun that tickle the ear,
And a paintbrush of chaos is always near.
Behind every beam, there's a joke to play,
With laughter ringing, come what may.

Memories linger in grins turned shy,
Bouncing back as the years go by.
The walls, our jokers, never unheard,
With a wink, they chuckle at every word.

Layers of Life Within

In layers thick, the stories thrive,
Captured moments, oh, how they arrive!
A scratch on the surface, a wink from the past,
In this funny guise, our giggles are cast.

Peeling back memories like skin of an onion,
Each laugh exposes more than a bunion.
A tickle in time where mismatched socks,
Tell of adventures 'round the blocks.

With every lift of the eyes around,
New jokes jump out, they're always found.
A tapestry woven with threads of delight,
Life's rich humor, a joyous sight.

So gather the echoes, the flickers of light,
In this charming maze, each corner feels right.
For within these layers, so spry and bold,
Lies the laughter in life's fabric, a joy to behold.

Echoes of Silent Stories

In corners hid the tales we know,
A sneaky mouse has stolen the show.
He giggles loud, runs fast, and squeaks,
Echoing laughter, the wall just peeks.

A creaky floor lets secrets out,
What old chairs whisper, they rave and shout.
A dusty clock ticks time away,
While shadows dance, they laugh and play.

The chandelier sways, a sprightly reveal,
It knows our dance, it knows the deal.
The basement's ghost is quite the hoot,
With silly hats and sparkling loot.

So if you listen, lend an ear,
These playful walls will bring you cheer.
For every scratch and every crack,
Tells a story, of joy and knack.

Whispers Beneath the Surface

Down in the cellar, the barrels talk,
They gossip 'bout folks who make a squawk.
Down with the dust, they have their fun,
Swapping tall tales till the day is done.

A low beam chirps, "Can't take that leap!"
While the rafters giggle, unable to sleep.
Their jests echo up through the cracks,
As spiders weave webs that don't cut slack.

The old rug chuckles, a fluffy delight,
Tripping the cat in its silly flight.
With each little scuffle, a raucous show,
The stories they share start to overflow.

So next time you visit, don't just glance,
Stand still in the chaos and join the dance.
For beneath the surface, when quiet freezes,
Lies a realm of whispers, oh how it pleases!

The Language of Shadows

In the hall, shadows twist and bend,
Laughter erupts—who knew they'd send?
A gnome in the corner preps for a jest,
In shades of gray, he's truly the best.

A shadowy cat sings a soft meow,
To a lamp on the wall, they take a bow.
"Let's dance!" they say, as forks do twirl,
A merry old waltz, such a fun swirl.

The floorboards creak, joining in on the fun,
With every step, they become one.
In the dim light, secrets unveil,
A silent bravado, a mirthful tale.

So next time you wander where no one treads,
Listen, and follow where humor leads.
For shadows can giggle and play all night,
In their silent, quirky, wondrous light.

Murmurs in the Masonry

The bricks have formed a merry band,
Chattering away, oh isn't it grand?
A crackling wall with a pun to share,
"Did you hear the one with the mouse and the hare?"

In the mortar, whispers spin like a dream,
Echoing laughter flows in a stream.
They jest about time, the wind, and the sun,
Arguing lightheartedly, just for fun.

The pillars hold court, with jokes up their sleeve,
As ivy creeps close, trying to believe.
With each little murmur, stories evoke,
Of all things jolly, they share their smoke.

So if you wander this hidden space,
Stop for a moment, join the embrace.
For the murmurs hold magic, a bright cheer spree,
In every whisper, a giggle's decree.

Memoirs in the Masons' Craft

In a corner, a brick thought it was neat,
To wear a hard hat and boots on its feet.
It built a small throne from the dust and the grime,
Declaring, "I'm king of this house, just in time!"

Chisel and hammer had a dance in the night,
They giggled and chuckled, oh, what a sight!
The mortar just sighed, with a grin on its edge,
'You boys need a break, or you'll fall off the ledge!'

A block made of marble said, "I'm so grand!"
While a silly old cobblestone said, "Just a strand!"
The bricks laughed and argued, who was the best,
The punchlines all landed, oh, what a jest!

As twilight descended, they held a debate,
The winner would get to decide on their fate.
But no one was listening, they just cracked up,
For laughter's the mortar that held them all up!

Footprints on the Forgotten

In a house with no roof, but a story quite loud,
Footprints jig and jive, they're a fun-loving crowd.
One wore a big hat, another had shoes,
Together they danced in a rhythm of blues!

The left feet were squeaky, the right ones just slipped,
They twirled and they whirled, not one moment skipped.
They'd hop on the floorboards and bounce off the walls,
Chasing each other like children in halls!

"Hey, can you hear us?" they shouted with glee,
"Footprints on a mission, just let us be free!"
The dust bunnies joined in, with a wiggle and flutter,
Creating a shoe store with a dash and a clutter!

But twilight came creeping, and they knew the end,
'Til the morning light called them out to descend.
With a wink and a giggle, they left a bright trail,
Promising next night they would dance without fail!

Tapestry of Time in Tumbledown

Threads of laughter woven through the old beams,
Tell tales of adventures and whimsical dreams.
A tapestry woven by grandmothers past,
While cats rolled right on it, purring at last!

A scrap of old fabric claimed it once flew,
A banner of victory, bright colors so true.
It meant to be noble, but now it just lays,
With a moth in the corner, dreaming of better days!

A needle and thread held a comical fight,
Stitching a laugh as they danced in twilight.
But snags in the yarn had them all in a mess,
"I'm tangled!" cried one, "What a stitchy distress!"

With giggles aplenty, they patched up the seams,
Creating a quilt made of playful daydreams.
For laughter's the thread that keeps growing in leaps,
Where the fabric of time eternally peeps!

Whispers from the Weathered

Old shutters creaked, like a gossipy friend,
Telling tales of the neighbors that never would end.
The roof shook and chuckled with every gust strong,
"Oh, listen up, humans, you've been here too long!"

The floorboards creaked softly, a snicker or two,
"Last week, I heard them, quite brazenly moo!"
A silly old fence chimed in with a grin,
"Did you see that bird? What a dive like a win!"

The paint peeled away, just to get a peek,
"Every crack in the wall has a story to speak!"
And the windows would wink, as they caught every glance,
While the house threw a party, everyone danced!

But the laughter grew quiet as dusk turned to night,
The whispers fell silent, all snuggled in tight.
Yet tomorrow would come, with new tales and delight,
Where the stories would mingle, and joy would ignite!

Stone Sagas

In the corner, a cat takes a nap,
While echoes of laughter fill the gap.
Bricks and mortar, they've heard it all,
Even the squeaky shoes, making a call.

A ghost with a grin, what a happy sight,
Telling tall tales by the pale moonlight.
Chasing shadows as old as the floor,
They crack a joke and then ask for more.

The windows giggle with sunlight beams,
As walls whisper softly, sharing dreams.
A patch of paint, chipped and sly,
Jests of the past, zipping by.

So gather around, for this house does know,
Every mishap, each little show.
In the bricks of the past, laughter does dwell,
In stone, oh, the stories they love to tell!

The Intimate Confessions of Ceilings

Up high on the ceiling, cobwebs do sway,
Listening close to the children at play.
Secrets they gather, night after night,
Whispered confessions in the soft twilight.

A light bulb flickers, with a cheerful dance,
It hears all the drama—oh, what a chance!
From feuds over dinner to giggles and cheers,
It knows the punchlines and stifles the tears.

Dust bunnies tumble, with a hop and a skip,
When dust motes take flight, it's a hilarious trip.
The ceiling just chuckles, for it sees all the fun,
A watchful companion, work never done.

So if you look up, give a wink and a smile,
The ceiling's been laughing all the while.
It holds every memory, light as a feather,
In the vastness above, stories come together.

Portraits of the Past Framed in Plaster

Framed in plaster, a grimace or two,
The portraits all gossip, it's wildly true.
With eyes full of mischief, they watch us below,
Scheming and dreaming, plotting the show.

A mustached man, so dignified,
Queries the cat, 'Did you dare to hide?'
The lady in lace stifles a laugh,
At the dog with the shoes—oh, what a gaffe!

With every stiff grin, tales unfold,
Of picnics gone wrong and secrets retold.
Old frames may be dusty, but their humor is bright,
They giggle with shadows in the dimming light.

So stop for a moment, take in their grace,
Each silly expression, every funny face.
For within these paintings, a comedy lives,
In the stillness of plaster, what joy it gives!

Silent Testimonies of the Facade

Oh, the facade, so proud and bold,
It's seen all the antics, stories untold.
From pranks in the garden to splashes of paint,
Each layer of history, a humorous saint.

With shutters that creak, like a laugh just begun,
It shares in the fun, like a bright summer sun.
A leaf caught in laughter, gently sways,
As the facade giggles through long summer days.

The porch swing sways like a child's delight,
Holding memories tight on those warm starry nights.
It cradles the whispers of parties once held,
Where the toast to mishaps was lovingly spelled.

As seasons change, stories continue to weave,
With every old chip, a new tale to conceive.
The facade stands tall, a witness to cheer,
In a world full of jest, its humor is clear.

Murals of Memory

A splatter of paint, a tale to tell,
In a corner where laughter once fell.
Old faces grin from the wall's embrace,
Caught forever in a funny place.

Worn bricks giggle with tales of cheer,
Of pizza parties and spilled chilled beer.
Each stroke a joke, a whimsical tease,
Faded fragments of moments that please.

The characters dance in colors so bright,
They jest and they jive, oh what a sight!
As I pass by, they nudge and they wink,
"Don't take life too serious, just pour another drink!"

With every glance, nostalgia knocks,
Echoes of laughter from painted blocks.
These murals hold secrets, both silly and grand,
In a gallery of giggles, so joyously planned.

Shadows of Old Footsteps

Footprints whisper along the ground,
Each step a jester in silence profound.
They shimmy and shake with comedic flair,
Leaving behind tales from the air.

Ghosts of pranks and puppets in flight,
Slipping on bananapeels in the twilight.
With a hop and a skip, they stroll down the lane,
Creating a spectacle of delight and disdain.

Every shadow has a story to spin,
Of playful chases and unlikely kin.
They trip on their own, or laugh 'til they cry,
As benches bear witness to jokes that flutter by.

In the twilight glow, they dash in the mist,
Making a spectacle, you wouldn't want to miss.
So step where they've danced, and join in the fun,
For shadows will giggle until the day's done.

The Archive of Abandoned Spaces

Dust bunnies gather in corners so shy,
They hold planning meetings and tell jokes on the fly.
Each forsaken room filled with whimsy and lore,
Laughter echoes lightly from one cracked door.

Old chairs tell secrets when nobody's around,
Of wild karaoke in a forgotten town.
With each creak and squeak, they share a good jest,
Encouraging echoes of fun-loving zest.

The windows are peeking with laughter and glee,
As squirrels share punchlines over cups of tea.
In forgotten spaces, the absurd comes alive,
Where the lost join the party and jive, jive, jive!

So wander through nooks that the world has ignored,
And find that the silly is never outscored.
Each dusty corner has stories that shine,
In the land of the funny, where whimsy is divine.

Notes from the Nooks

Hidden in crevices, laughter is penned,
Notes from the nooks where the silly descend.
With paper airplanes and origami laughs,
Messages linger in quirky paths.

"I've lost my marbles!" shouts one little note,
While another declares, "The cat stole my coat!"
Written in crayon and smudged with a grin,
Each slip of paper is a cheeky win.

The corners start chuckling, a giggly parade,
As forgotten scribbles weave tales of charades.
"Did you hear about Charlie? He danced with a broom!
While the old couch has dreams of escaping the room!"

So unfold the treasures with spontaneity's flair,
For the whispers of humor are hidden everywhere.
In nooks, they abound—an unfinished tale,
With each folded corner, let laughter prevail!

Voices Hidden in the Grain

In the silence of wood, laughter does play,
Knots in the timber, they tell tales all day.
Squeaks and creaks, a jig on the floor,
Whispers of ghosts who just want to score.

A cabinet chuckles, it's got stories galore,
Of socks that went missing, and ketchup on the floor.
The chair tells that tale of the cat's wild ballet,
While the old table grins, it still loves a buffet.

A shelf with a secret, a diary in dust,
With dreams of adventure, oh it's a must!
The beams hold some gossip, but who keeps a score?
Of all the odd things living, one never gets bored.

So listen closely, when you're home all alone,
For all these old things have got humor, well-known.
In the heart of the timber, the memories drip,
With laughter and joy, take a moment to sip.

Secrets Embedded in Stone

In the cracks of the walls, jokes are displayed,
A mischievous stone likes to play charade.
With a wiggle and twist, it giggles out loud,
The bricks form a chorus, quite silly and proud.

A pebble once stole a the rock's parking spot,
And the wall painted whispers of who likes what.
Moss joins the fun with a dance so divine,
As the granite shimmers, it's all by design.

The arches have punchlines that never fall flat,
While the old window grins at the cat wearing hats.
Each stone has a tale, some too wild to repeat,
While the laughter of nature makes life feel complete.

So listen for echoes, those giggles in stone,
The humor of history is never alone.
With secrets and smiles, let the fun be your guide,
In a world full of whimsy, there's joy to confide.

Tales of the Timeless Structure

Oh sturdy old structure, with a wink in your frame,
You've seen all the shenanigans, life's funny game.
The roof has a joke that it tells to the sky,
While the doors creak along, as if joining the high!

Balconies chuckle as people pass by,
With each little bump, they seem to sigh.
The stairs have a rhythm, a tap and a hop,
It's a ballet of laughter, we find it hard to stop.

Each room holds a quip, a chuckle or two,
While the hallways giggle at all that we do.
Light fixtures flicker, like they're part of the show,
With laughter surrounding, there's always the glow.

So dwell in this haven of jest and delight,
Where the tales of the structure bring smiles to the night.
In this timeless old place, let humor stand tall,
For in every nook, there's a giggle for all.

The Heartbeat of Brick and Mortar

In the pulse of the bricks, there's a rhythm so sweet,
With footsteps and giggles, it dances on its feet.
Mortar holds secrets, and bricks have some sass,
As the wall cracks a smile, oh time likes to pass.

The chimney cracks jokes, it's a real stand-up act,
While windows are peeking, they're always intact.
With laughter that echoes through openings wide,
Each room's an ensemble, so much joy and pride.

The foundation chuckles, sturdy and strong,
While ceilings hum soft, like a comforting song.
In the laughter of brick and the warmth of the core,
There's a tale to be told, who could ask for more?

So listen intently, let the fun draw you near,
For laughter is vibrant, it lingers right here.
In the heart of each building, there's joy to be found,
With the heartbeat of humor, it's endlessly sound.

www.ingramcontent.com/pod-product-compliance
Lightning Source LLC
Chambersburg PA
CBHW060135230426
43661CB00003B/430